So...

for

Classical Stars

Julian Morgan

ISBN: 9781731230416

Edition 1.0.0

All of the artwork used in this book
was created by Julian Morgan

Any errors or omissions in this book are
the fault of the author. They will be rectified
as soon as he becomes aware of them.

Please email with any requests for improvements
or corrections and if your suggestions are acted upon,
your name will be added on to the list on
the Acknowledgements page.

DEDICATION

For Cindy

ACKNOWLEDGEMENTS

My thanks go to all who helped in making
suggestions or in checking the manuscript of this book,
especially John Bird, Hugh Cooke and Joka Morgan.

CONTENTS

Introduction

Sonnets for Classical Stars is a companion volume to my earlier book, *Sonnets for Yorkshire Stars.* There has been no particular reason for writing this book beyond the fact that I enjoy writing this sort of poem very much and have sought and found pleasure from bringing aspects of people's lives from the ancient world into the medium.

As I have written before, the sonnet has been widely used in the English language as a poetic form to express love or admiration and this is certainly the purpose of the ones I have written here. In this case, however, perhaps that admiration is aimed as much at the cultures and civilisations involved as at the individuals who are the subjects of the poems. After all, once can't *really* admire Zeus, can one?

In fourteen lines, there is a limit to how much one can say but it has been an exciting and rewarding challenge to meet. For those keen-eyed readers whose interest in poetic structure needs to be addressed, I will happily admit that while most of the sonnets here are Shakespearean in form, there are a couple included which break the Bard's rules.

My selection of Classical stars has been made without any great system or purpose. You will find characters from myths and legends here alongside literary and historical figures. The four sections of the book will give it some sort of structure, though I do hope its random element will continue to maintain some of its authenticity.

Julian Morgan
www.yorkshireauthor.com

Agamemnon

Stars

of

Sagas &

Stories

Achilles

When Thetis took the baby, dipped him in
        And murky Stygian waters swirled around,
The son of Peleus (happily no kin
Of Zeus) held by dry ankle, never drowned.

So nothing then could touch him, nothing harm,
Intact he'd be 'gainst every sort of blow.
At least he'd get the fame and no alarm,
If under fire from Hector he should go.

He gave old Agamemnon loads of stick
When once the girl Briseis he'd demand.
Refused to fight there, even in the thick
Of Greek friends being wiped out on Trojan sand.

Once Hector slew his friend, his words repealed.
Then Paris pricked him, took him in dry heel.

Aeneas

When Troy once fell, its people facing end,
Great Hector came before him in a dream.
Get up and go! Our folks on you depend!
Then Venus and Creusa confirmed theme.

He left the fiery towers and sailed away,
Old lad aloft and young one holding hand.
Their ships were wrecked, dad died, and Dido's way
Was had: once in the cave, he'd not withstand.

My man! That's what *she* thought! Our gallant friend
Saw diff'rent meanings there in lover's tryst.
She gave up hope. Her final dividend
A pyre, when checked-out lover, abject, missed.

Our hero made it through, Italian land;
Though weight of Dido's curse his people damned.

Agamemnon

Mycenae's king, he led the Greeks to Troy,
Though only after very *Iffy* start,
When taught by Calchas vileness to deploy
In Aulis, where young daughter broke his heart.

A thousand ships he led to Dardan lands,
Where Greeks and Trojans fought it out ten years,
Where brother Menelaus on those sands
Restored to Spartan Helen her frontiers.

It seemed the mighty king had overcome
All challenges he'd faced from foreign foes.
Well, Clytemnestra knew still what he'd done:
What Clytemnestra planned, he'd not foreclose.

When mighty kings mistake, their wives neglect,
The bath's a dangerous place to recollect.

Ajax

The mighty fall, it's tragedy's motif,
    As Ajax with his towering shield makes clear.
So when Achilles fell, Odysseus thief
Became, in our man's eyes, of arms so dear.

Once madness came, Athena's guarantee
That sheep and cattle, bloody, met their end,
There in the tent, the warrior's shame to see
Would blight his glory, suicide portend.

Tecmessa begged to no avail, *Relent
And still stand tall,* though Ajax persevered,
Dejected by his blade, in deep dissent:
Half-brother Teucer's late and swathed in tears.

Our lesson from this sorry tale, in brief?
The mighty fall, it's tragedy's motif.

Cassandra

Apollo's not an easy chap to cheat,
　　Though when he makes a promise, can't go back.
Well when Cassandra said with him she'd meet,
He offered prophecy, once in the sack.

The trouble was, she thought again, refused:
The archer god was really very miffed.
His anger only then could be diffused
By making sure that none would catch her drift.

So if she said the end was nigh, deaf ears
Would hear the words but never quite believe.
Although poor Priam's daughter shed some tears,
Enlightenment for Trojans, unachieved.

Anticipated Greek King's bloody bath,
Before she fell to royal psychopath.

Clytemnestra

With High King Agamemnon on campaign
   To free her sister Helen, bring her back,
Abandoned Clytemnestra's grudge remained;
Iphigenia's loss would have payback.

Now after long and sore deliberation,
She picked Aegisthus as her running mate.
Their target was to wreak retaliation:
Her man's return they'd eagerly await.

She laid red carpet down for him to tread,
Beguiled and said the bath was nicely hot.
Ten years away and he was thinking, *Bed!*
He'd wash the dust off first, then hit the spot.

Presuming on a promise, caked in mud,
Wife swung the axe, the waters swirled with blood.

Coriolanus

From captured Corioli's appellation,
　　Our erstwhile hero had a height to fall.
He'd been the people's darling, won the nation,
　　Though suspect tribunes feared the tyrant's thrall.

When paucity of grain was hurting hard,
Then Marcius lent his efforts to propound,
To cast down one-time champion and safeguard,
To drive to exile, drive to Volscian ground.

He led their foes against them, raised the stakes
As five miles short of city, drew his lines.
When wife Volumnia's tears put on the brakes,
Self-exiled husband halted his designs.

To Volscian foe was brought back Roman odium;
The payment for his toil? Blood in Antium.

Dido

Sychaeus fell before Pygmalion's sword
    And Tyrian Elissa had to split.
Iarbas made the Libyan sand award:
With oxhide-con, the king she would outwit.

She laid out Carthage, built the great foundations,
As Trojan on his travels paused for breath.
Then, in the cave, shared lusty consummations,
Inevitably leading to her death.

Aeneas sailed away; though sad, not set
To stay, cast as the husband of a Queen.
On Dido's pyre her curse usurped regret;
For desert sorrows, Punic wars laid scene.

They met in Hades: speechless, wouldn't look
On him but to Sychaeus herself took.

Hector

The bravest of the fifty Trojan sons,
He struggled hard to save his native soil.
His father Priam knew he wouldn't run;
Away from Greek attacks, he'd not recoil.

Achilles was the only one he'd meet
In battle's chaos, more than him serene.
Achilles was the one he'd not defeat,
Though in that armour Patroclus seemed keen.

When tied behind the wheels, his dusty corpse
Bumped blackened round the battered walls of Troy.
When father to his foe's tent took recourse,
Achilles was the one who'd give back boy.

Astyanax, his son, feared nodding plume:
Andromache, his wife, smiled on, though doomed.

Helen

The face that launched a thousand ships, *they say,*

    Though other folks might see it differently.

The hussy dumped her husband, ran away,

Sought life on Trojan shores across the sea.

In ancient tales it's never quite so plain:

The oath Tyndareus placed as binding vow

Would never let the other Greeks abstain

From promise made, would never disallow.

When Paris gave the golden fruit to her,

Glad Aphrodite knew what she was at.

She knew of Menelaus, knew it blurred,

It wasn't Helen's fault that she'd fall flat.

Blame Helen if you like, I'll not pick cudgels.

But others share the blame for Trojans' struggles.

Horatius

Etruscans under Lars Porsena raged
   While Romans thought up ways to face their foe,
All banded by the river's edge, unfazed,
Prepared to cross the Tiber, stage their show.

Horatius, Larcius and Herminius
Arose and strode forth, raising lusty shouts,
They chopped and lopped at bridge's timber struts
To snatch their path from cross Etruscan louts.

As axes raised and felled Sublician piers,
The King of Clusium grimaced at the sight.
While Roman trio whittled on, his fears
Were nourished, stuffed and swollen at Rome's might.

The tumbling timbers tottered, wherewithal,
Horatius took the current, swimming crawl.

Lesbia

You, sexy lady, brought down to his knees
Verona poet-lad, too soft for you.
You led him on with dubious expertise
Of love and all its ways, though not virtue.

It started out a long electric gaze:
He thrilled to see you, catch when you would throw
Some little scraps to tempt in mist and haze.s
Poor spaniel fool, who'd never truly know.

Then once his sparrow-lust had passed, his rage
Would batter at his soul and not relent.
Those curses hurled at you writ on the page
As love turned round to hatred and torment.

We think that you were Clodia, wrecked his life:
The courtroom lawyer's bane, Metellus' wife.

Lucretia

What virtue was, was the debate that night,
When Collatinus drank with Sextus T.
They rode back home and found to his delight
Lucretia at her loom, a sight to see.

Then dreams took hold of Sextus; he'd possess
The girl who'd seemed so welcoming and mild.
Returning, forced himself on her, pressed threats
And then his friend betrayed, his wife defiled.

Once overwhelmed by rape and breach of trust,
She knew she couldn't live with that; her life
Surrendered in her father's arms, she thrust
Down deep in noble breast a noble knife.

What virtue was, was clear when finally shown;
When Brutus cast the Tarquins out of Rome.

Lupa

A howling wolf in Latin's most unclear:
Could just as easy mean a prostitute.
So Lupa's quite a tricky name to hear,
And trickier still true role to attribute.

Once, Rhea Silvia's boys were born to Mars,
When golden showers didn't mean the same.
Though hid away, a Vestal, behind bars,
He got to her and played his naughty game.

Old evil uncle cast them all away.
By river's edge, the Tiber, they were found.
Though who it was who saved them, hard to say,
The twins were taken off to higher ground.

Now were they *really* suckled on wolf's milk?
Did Lupa *really* nourish Roman ilk?

Lysistrata

In desperate times there's measures matching them
    Which give the means to quell an aroused state.
Lysistrata had tricky trials for men:
Persuaded pals they wouldn't meet to mate.

The women sat on the Acropolis;
Cut off the flow of cash to fund the war.
They all would strive to save metropolis,
The ladies holding back, a me-too corps.

The fight's too long, too harsh, too dear, too cruel:
She'd stop the skirmish any way she could.
Men's angry flames fell once they failed in fuel,
Their poles projecting out like hardened wood.

So next time that you think to make some peace,
Remember this. Don't fight for your release.

Medea

Medea's help won Jason Golden Fleece,
When dragon's teeth were sown in Colchis sod.
The combat-crop reduced with ointment's grease,
She sailed away, while slicing brother's bod.

Her father stopped to gather up the bits
All scattered, bloody, on the foaming surf.
And though departed daughter kept her wits,
Disloyal Jason lost his, strayed from turf.

In Corinth, Creon offered him new wife
To ease his troubles, thinking Colchis nought.
Medea saw revenge and took her knife;
In spite, her children killed, a fresh onslaught.

So if you want a fleece, don't make It golden,
Or else to wicked witch might be beholden.

Minos

When Minos got his gift, Poseidon's bull,
The only job for him to carve a slice
Through victim's neck, he really couldn't pull
It off. In face of slaughter... just too nice.

Well then the trident god had fiendish plan
And Pasiphaë felt a strange love call.
She saw the taurine huge as fancy man
As suddenly his hooves began to maul.

He had his way, the lowering mighty beast,
Though Mrs Minos knew it wasn't right.
Her husband's reward, courage now decreased
Beside of problems in palatial blight.

To keep the dreadful freak from foreign gaze,
Hired Daedalus to hide him, build a maze.

Odysseus

Pretending madness didn't cut the mustard,
    When Palamedes gave the game away.
Odysseus went to Troy once he was busted:
For home, for twenty years or so, he'd pray.

Those wheezes that he dreamed, you'd not surpass:
He slipped and slithered, even in a pickle.
The wooden horse, the sirens' wax and mast;
He kept his cool, though comrades often fickle.

Well when the time came for his homely test,
The suitors all lined up to knock him down.
Resisting bow would stop them and attest
To master of the house, who shot them down.

The final proof and final challenge, when
He couldn't move the bed for dear old Pen.

Oedipus

Before his birth a ghastly tale had told
    Of things so awful, parents cast him out
With feet tied up and shivering in the cold:
His nemesis was never in much doubt.

So when he met his dad where three roads met,
The old chap didn't really have a chance.
Then on to Thebes where Queen Jocasta's debt
Was paid in full, when he solved sphinx's rants.

Teiresias tried hard to show the truth,
When tangled words from Delphi Creon brought.
But Oedipus had none of it. Uncooth,
He threatened holy man whose help he'd sought.

He never saw before, when he was sighted.
He came to see, once blindness left benighted.

Pandora

Prometheus:	The sacrifice is ready. Which part's yours?
Zeus:	I'll take the best bits. Tell me, which are they?
Prometheus:	I think, the meat's a really dreadful bore.
Zeus:	Well you keep that, put bones and fat my way...

Later

Zeus:	That Forethought chap's a stinker, knicked the meat!
Hera:	It's how to get him back though, that's the thing.
Hephaestus:	I'll make a special lady his conceit.
Athena:	I'll breathe on her and into life she'll spring...

Zeus:	He'll never fall for it. Let's try his bro.
Hera:	That Afterthought? You sure he's thick enough?
Zeus:	We'll give her gifts of heaven so he'll forgo.
Hera:	And box brimful with all the nasty stuff!

Later

Epimetheus:	Please don't look in the box, dear. That's a nope.
Pandora:	A lovely box, a little look?

Later

... Still hope.

Pelops

From rotten eggs bad smells do emanate
    And Pelops had a dad who qualified.
When Tantalus made stew, he'd macerate
His son, all chopped to bits and liquefied.

The gods who saw held back, though there was one
Who tried a bit of shoulder in her grief.
With iv'ry reassembled, boy was done:
Bad dad in Hades never got relief.

Well wheels turn better when they're kept secure
And axle pins are pretty good at that.
In Pelops' nobbled race, the win assured.
No axle pins? Her daddy's cart went splat.

From rotten eggs bad smells do emanate
As Pelops' sons would later simulate.

Priam

A king with fifty sons? And daughters too?
He had some busy nights, I dare suppose.
Well, goodness knows how Hecuba came through,
Exhausted from all those endless afterglows.

Mind you, I'm hardly jealous: he seemed doomed
To witness Trojans suffer Greek attacks,
To see the Spartan Helen all perfumed,
To watch his walls ablaze as city sacked.

With Hector at the front there in the ranks,
Deiphobus and Paris lurk behind.
Cassandra's saying stuff but no one thanks
Her for advice, which really they should mind.

Achilles' tent saw old man on his knees.
Achilles' son the old man, bloody, siezed.

Romulus

It's bad when brothers quarrel. Families!
  Who'd have one? Numitor was cursed, it seems.
His daughter's brood got scuppered in the sleaze:
Amulius and his ambitious dreams!

Well she-wolf saw and she-wolf fed the twins,
Though mum would fade away in Tiber's arms.
But brothers' curse would fall again on kin
When Romulus and Remus set alarms.

The omens seen, the walls were built, right there:
Where Palatine was choice of number one.
But second sibling's sighting, hardly fair,
Gave cause: the fratricidal deed was done.

Now Rome's first king was brother who killed brother,
First family of kings - and what a pother.

Theseus

The boy in Troizen couldn't lift the rock;
  Kept trying though, until the day once came,
It moved at last and then he had a shock:
The sword and sandals there would change his game.

He left for Athens on the bad, bad road
Where folks got stretched and chopped and cleaved by trees.
What Scyron, Sinon and Procustes owed,
He took from them, their trunks and limbs as fees.

Then came to court where poison cup quite failed:
Medea couldn't harm Aegeus' son.
He sailed to Crete, kept promising fresh sails
When work to kill the Minotaur was done.

But what you say you'll do is oft forgot:
His dad saw son's dark shroud and then he dropped.

Athena

Stars

of

Sanctuaries &

Shrines

Aphrodite

When Kronos cut, his dad's great gonads fell
Down into sea, all foaming round with blood.
Then, in the crimson spume, the ruddy swell,
Rose sexy Aphrodite out from flood.

Once blacksmith husband spotted her in bed
With mighty god of war, all wrapped in lust.
He cast a net above, a meshed bedspread,
For other gods to mock them, trapped and trussed.

Gold apple's mine, she thought, when Eris came,
Though both the others disagreed with her.
Her bribe of Helen landed Paris fame,
When Spartan queen to Trojan team transferred.

Son, archer Eros, fires unerring bow.
When victims feel his prick, it's all they'll know.

Apollo

Once Zeus walked out, the Titan girl's girth grew,
　　But parturition's tough when Hera's mad.
So Leto looked for place right out of view
And Delos was the land first saw this lad.

His beauty, music, potent healing, prized,
Though plague was also archer's special thing.
And Phoebus' bright sun's rays would catalyse
Prophetic wisdom, darkness lightening.

He downed the dragon by Parnassus sheer,
Then made the Pythian's place there to atone.
With games, oracular replies unclear,
Apollo's fabled Delphi stood alone.

When baby Hermes came and pinched his herd,
He took the lyre, to lessen guilt incurred.

Artemis

A pollo's sister stood in stream one day:
When Actaeon mistook, he saw her showered;
Infuriated goddess: well, he'd pay!
Transformed to stag and then by dogs devoured.

As victims of this chaste and angry mistress
Adonis and Orion fell foul too;
Poor Agamemnon, forced by calm at Aulis,
His little daughter pitiless would view.

The Romans called their Artemis Diana,
Whose help at childbirth ladies often sought.
With hunting dogs and arrows in her quiver,
Ephesians statues, multi-breasted, wrought.

At Brauron, little girls would dress as bears,
To honour virgin huntress's affairs.

Athena

A most unusual birth, from daddy's pate;
    You sprang, full-formed, alert and spear so stout,
With shield supported, helmet fixed in place.
Amazing how that kit could all come out!

Contending with Poseidon for the town,
The olive tree you furnished took the prize.
The Periclean Parthenon's renown
Has kept your name forever from demise.

The scary aegis, hanging from your arm,
Was once a part of gorgon's ghastly face.
Her skin's a dreadful paralysing charm
Which turns to stone, as foes their fear embrace.

You, owl-eyed goddess Pallas, so astute,
Were even the inventor of the flute.

Cupid

When silly Psyche's oil drop startled him,
The son of Venus knew she'd work things out.
Don't ever look, he'd told her, verbatim,
Lie down, enjoy our lusty bout. Don't doubt!

His arrows hadn't failed right up until
He pricked himself by chance and gazed on her.
Love at first sight he knew, before that spill
Would drive dejection on their whisperers.

I never really know if Cupid's one
Or many. Goldsmiths on Pompeian walls
Tell tales of tiny cauldron-stirring fun;
Fore-runners of Baroque in painted halls.

Know this: if arrow strikes, you'll be consumed:
His piercing shaft once in you, then you're doomed.

Dionysus

The eager panthers run beside his car;
His wavy hair cascades about those cheeks;
The wine cup in his hand, his ivied spar
In little squares shows wine-god's wild techniques.

That's Bacchic Dionysus' ecstasy;
The Satyrs and those Maenads take part too.
They celebrate the son of Semele,
Whom Zeus's thigh once held, when lightning flew.

The nymphs of Nysa nurtured fledgling boozer
Who'd come to Greece to win acceptance there.
But when poor Pentheus took him for a loser,
Had harsh revenge on uncle unaware.

Well, next time you take vino, just think on:
You're worshipping the wine-god - called upon.

Heracles

The son of Zeus annoyed his old dad's wife;
    Just by his birth he'd underlined the fact
That Queen of Heaven's rivals were too rife.
Alcmena's son would see his troubles stacked.

It started right away, when serpents sent
To infiltrate his cradle got a hold.
He strangled would-be stranglers in attempt:
Well, after that, few others made so bold.

Nemean lion's adamantine hide
Became his trademark after early hit.
Along with club to cosh held by his side;
First superhero's very basic kit.

Eurystheus King of Tiryns, mortified,
Jumped in his jar from hell-hound, petrified.

Hermes

Day one: Arcadian baby nicked some cows;
All fifty, took them in reverse for luck;
Then slaughtered two and in their entrails browsed,
And from their guts, guitar strings pulled to pluck.

If that's not bad enough, his soundbox frame
Was fashioned from dead tortoise carapace.
Yet when the son of Maia got the blame,
Half-brother, bribed with lyre, forgave disgrace.

A clever villain this and loved by thieves;
Commended, sought by merchants, tricksters too.
Escorted souls when time it was to leave:
The Underworld the place he'd pull them through.

He wore a cap and special wingèd shoes;
Held staff aloft where magic could perfuse.

Juno

When Dido's Carthage saw its walls rise high,
  Protecting Juno seemed the queen's best bet.
But when those pesky Trojan folks came by,
That bulwark failed her, much to her regret.

She'd raised the storm and ripped their fleet apart,
Persuaded old Aeolus to engage:
Her machinations devious and smart,
Before her brother Neptune stilled the waves.

While Dido's curses could not be misheard,
Aeneas sailed for settled Roman life.
Juno changed her mind, her memories blurred
Of Paris on Mount Ida, apple-strife.

Fertility and parturition's friend,
The Romans prayed this queen for happy end.

Jupiter

The sky, the lightning flashes and the rain,
 All made the Romans want to sacrifice
To great Olympian Lord, to ascertain
If Juno's cheating hubby would be nice.

The god of state, he helped them win their wars:
As *Stator* stopped the Sabines in their ranks,
When Romulus and Tatius gave him cause:
The Roman built a temple then for thanks.

The generals gave him spoils, if they earned,
And set up forum temples, his and hers:
To Capitol ambitious Tarquin turned,
The best and biggest godhead then referred.

But when the eagle flew out with the lad,
It wasn't best intentions: they were bad.

Mars

The god of war, who fathered Rhea's twins,
Had altar set nearby in his own field.
Where Romans came and prayed to save their skins,
To fight the foe and win and never yield.

There's love and war and in those ancient times,
They thought that Mars had met his loving match,
When Venus came a-calling oftentimes:
With cupids all around, she was a catch!

Augustus built a temple to define
His vengeful force as Roman quality.
Where Juno's son was seen to them benign,
Though heaven help the ones who'd disagree.

Today his planet, red, glows from afar,
Named after god of war, a Roman star.

Mithras

I stand beside the Wall at Carrawburgh,
And marvel at the temple aisle I see:
Projecting from the earth, the stones so rough,
Connecting with the god of truth for me.

Once born from giant egg in mystic start,
He grew to slay the bull with helping crew:
A scorpion, dog and serpent all took part,
To bring the beast right down and then undo.

The soldiers came here, sat upon this bench,
To worship him, to take part in his rites.
On ladder of his grades themselves entrenched,
From Crow to Father, bathing in his light.

The temple, like a cave of mysteries,
Sends mirages from times gone by to me.

Persephone

 racetrack now, where once Demeter's girl

Would run around and pick the pretty flowers.

Her Uncle Hades took her there, the churl,

From Enna's meadows to his deathly bower.

If only pomegranate in her hands

Was no temptation for the lass! Six seeds

She ate, so six months yearly stays from lands,

While crops won't grow and all that's left's rank weeds.

The Underworld's a dark and gloomy place,

Though once you're there, there's not much chance to leave.

Demeter's daughter's one who can efface

Its shades and rise above, six months retrieve.

Persephone's half years still alternate,

So seeds of grain in soil can germinate.

Pluto

There's names aplenty for the Lord below,
Whose lot fraternal's empire of the Dead.
Try Hades, Dis, Plouton or yet Pluto:
We all must meet him, once a cut in thread.

But first we have to get across the Styx,
With grim old Charon on his creaky raft.
There's Aeacus and Cerberus to fix,
The guardians Pluto keeps on hellish staff.

Now if you're good, he'll send you to the top;
Elysium's a pretty place to be.
But if you're not, he'll seal your doom. You'll drop
Right down to Tartarus, your penalty.

Propitiate? Pick beast? What kind? Jet black
Will do. Just once. You won't be coming back.

Poseidon

O dysseus poked his son in bloody eye,
   So blinded Polyphemus fumbled round;
Then prayed to sea-god father, *Rectify!*
Don't let him back to Ithaca undrowned!

Poseidon's rage aroused, made manifest,
The waves at wandering hero did incite.
Phaeacian sand saw stumbling and undressed,
A handball game conceded at the sight.

Athena's gain it was, his Attic loss;
Though when Troy fell at last, he got his way.
The serpents snared the priest who called him boss;
His homage unacknowledged on that day.

When once the shaker's trident struck the main,
The journey home for victims, cruel strain.

Poseidon

Pythia

hey came from all across the world to ask
Her Delphic help, which most would fail to heed:
All couched in verse and riddles, like a mask,
Concealing meaning, all in words she'd read.

Castalian spring her waters brought, so clear,
Unlike those prophecies that Pythia gave.
In navel of the earth she'd engineer
To give replies and answers that they'd crave.

She sat above the chasm by the rocks,
Where eagles soared and swooped right overhead.
Apollo's voicebox, hardly orthodox,
Was never clear but always right in thread.

Though *Know Yourself* above the door was writ,
There's not much more for sure that I'd submit.

Vesta

In Vesta's temple, Roman fires stayed lit
The whole year round or bad luck badgered them.
For pure attendants, thirty year remit
To live for her and keep away from men.

They brought her sacred salt cakes out at feasts,
Saw to it that the fire would always burn;
They followed the instructions of the priests.
In chastity, all other men would spurn.

On New Year's Day, they'd let the fire subside;
Rekindled it with twigs and sacred sticks.
That's March, you know, in case you can't decide,
Before our modern calendar got fixed.

The stone from Troy conserved inside by them:
Palladium's the name, their lucky gem.

Zeus

Had Kronos chewed his food, he would have yelped
    On stubbing teeth and spitting out great stone,
Which Rhea substituted for her whelp,
Who set it up in Delphi, once he'd grown.

When Zeus exsected siblings from dad's gut,
It proved prophetic warnings can't be stalled.
He drew the lots with brothers for his cut,
Then made himself Olympian Lord of all.

Defeated Titans, Giants in great strife,
With thunderbolts resounding up on high.
He took his grumpy sister as his wife;
When Hera nagged, he'd rumble in the sky.

I only have one word for you to brood:
Just take good care you always chew your food.

Stars
of
Skill &
Style

Homer

Aeschylus

This writer's Fate, relentless and unbowed,
    Would cast both kings and heroes from their path.
Cassandra's crazy nonsense foretold loud
Poor slaughtered Agamemnon in the bath.

Orestes? Vengeance drove to leave a tress:
On father's tomb, Electra saw the braid.
Aegisthus, Clytemnestra fell. Obsessed,
The Furies tracked who'd called on father's shade.

Athenian staunch, he fought to take the day
Against the Persian foe at Marathon,
Then thirteen times the prize took for his plays:
With high-flown compounds, theatre's paragon.

By Gela's marge when eagle thought his pate
A rock, a high-flown tortoise dropped. Prostrate.

Archimedes

This scientist, all cylinders and spheres,
Invented more than most in Syracuse.
He's famous for his screw. Well! Pioneers
In water tech and pumps of sorts enthuse.

He solved all kinds of stuff, not least the crown,
Which Syracusan king thought falsified.
He dipped it in a bowl, then called it *found*!
Displacement **and** the gold identified.

Then when Marcellus and the Roman troops
Came threatening to conquer his home town,
His answer was a claw to raise their poops:
Unbalancing astern should take them down.

When Cicero once found obscured enclave,
A cylinder and sphere still marked his grave.

Aristophanes

Once fakes and phoneys dominate the scene
  And politicians fail to see it right,
You know that satire's going to bite, demean,
Exaggerate those failings and indict.

Old Attic jokes were just like ours, you know:
Read Aristophanes, you'll find that's true.
For Cleon came a Babylonian blow;
The jurors in the Wasps got rumbled too.

Socratic nonsense spoofed and mocked in Clouds,
As wise man's basket floated all around.
Lysistrata left furrows quite unploughed,
With rampant, sex-starved husbands beaten down.

His greatest gags and giggles? In the Frogs,
In Dionysus' hellish dialogues.

Aristotle

Philosophers came thick and fast those days,
    Though this one dwarfed the others' repertoires.
Colossal output: science and mores;
Lyceum's founder, ex-Platonic star.

Those -*ologies* abounded on his lists,
With *philo-*, *theo-*, *bio-* at the front.
The Unmoved Mover and his untaught trysts
A constant source of questions in his hunt.

If you have things you'd like to classify,
He got there first, I'd guess; that was his game.
His Final Cause perhaps you'd ratify,
Along with observation, you'd acclaim.

Need Logic, Ethics, Physics, Politics?
They're all in Aristotle's bag of tricks.

Catullus

It's Lesbia who did for you, young man.
That girl who teased, seduced and took you out.
Her true, her Clodian name you wouldn't tout
In Sapphic-styled production. Lustful plan.

Though where and when and why it all began
I couldn't speculate: there is no doubt
That mixed emotions, love and hatred's pout
Would pit despair on hopeful, sparrow-man.

If only Garda's lake had seen you stay,
Those crazy ups and downs were not your norm;
Enchanted no, nor branded by that blaze.

You came to Rome from foaming Adige,
Tormented from Verona: you reformed
The songs of Greece, encased in Latin ways.

Cicero

N ew man, he boasted, *Did it on my own:*
He called himself *PP*, Rome's great papa.
A modest man? Not likely! And he'd moan
In exile, when by Clodius disbarred.

But don't disparage Cicero too much:
He really was a special kind of chap.
The young man taking on Chrysogonus
Was brave to challenge Sulla, take the rap.

Sicilian extortion seemed alright
To those of Verres' class who'd sent him there.
The prosecuting lawyer's courtroom fight
Secured redress and new provincial care.

Octavian (for shame!) cut through the great
Man's cord, hands tied, through fear of advocate.

Cicero

Empedocles

There's earth, there's air, there's fire and water too.
That's all there is around us, so he told.
It's from those elements that all things grew:
That's everything, in nature manifold.

Then love and strife are things to bind and flit,
As magnets, pull and push their like away.
The four component elements permit
All life forms to evolve and to decay.

Empedocles it was, who gave us this,
The presocratic chap from Acragas.
The scientist and poet gave a miss;
When tyrant's chair fell empty, he said *Pass*.

Philosopher, who fell in Etna's bowl,
Down in the crater's deep, dark steamy hole.

Euripides

When noble themes and lofty odes were key,
His beggars, women, thieves and slaves too new
For leading parts in plays. His tragedy,
His sitcom style, berated ballyhoo.

Medea was the bitch we'd understand,
When faced by Jason's glib and barefaced lies.
Hippolytus found Phaedra underhand:
No love, no lust, no rape, no compromise.

While peeping Pentheus met his sordid side,
The wine-god drove his mum Agave mad.
His head, cut off and brandished far and wide;
Though Cadmus couldn't help, poor old grandad.

The playwright died in Macedonian court;
Got torn apart by dogs, said the report.

Herodotus

That traveller chap, the father of history?
A Carian Greek and rather a mystery...

Loved all his travels from Halicarnassus,
Watched things unravel en route for Parnassus.

Followed the Persians around in their wars,
Noted incursions, enquired for the cause.

Marathon running and Hellespont crossing,
Xerxes in torment and Darius bossing.

Down the Nile's delta he sailed on his quest.
Desert heat, sweltered, found crocodiles best.

Egyptian mummies? Found fun just to look:
Embalmed in their tummies, debrained with a hook.

So, thanks to Herodotus. Great account!
You gave the lot to us straight, paramount.

Hesiod

Boeotian boy, who gave us Works and Days,
 An epic hit of labours and of luck,
His brother Perses held full in his gaze,
Whose deal with dad's estate was badly struck.

He heard the Muses call on Helicon,
When shepherding his flock on mountainside.
He promised then and there he'd go full on;
Himself to sing and honour gods applied.

The Chaos he described was genesis
Of all that came thereafter, in a word.
With gods and titans, fighting all amiss;
Theogony, in places, quite absurd.

He made Prometheus once steal fire for men,
Then lose his liver, all pecked out again.

Hippocrates

Most times you'd swear an oath, you'd then be blamed
For being rude, offending others there.
But when you go for his one, you're acclaimed:
New doctor in new medical affair.

His sanctuary on Kos is where folks met
From all across the Greek and Roman sphere,
To seek Asclepius, ask his help and get,
For arm or leg or chest or eye or ear.

Hippocrates the healer wasn't all:
His promises kept poorly folks secure.
When in their houses doctors came to call,
They'd know their secrets would be kept, for sure.

So thanks to him for doctor's plighted troth
And trust, from swearing Hippocratic Oath.

Homer

The greatest and the first of all who wrote,
Was he a blind man, Chian, or a she?
We'll never really know, so make your vote
And play your part in timeless mystery.

What's sure is, there are stories, epic tales,
Of Troy, its walls, Odysseus and his men.
It's certain someone wrote them, though details
Are scarce of where and why and how and when.

If Homer was a man, a travelling bard
In Bronze Age times, he'd know the stuff reviewed.
But Dark Age makes an explanation hard:
Rejecting oral transfer, you'd be screwed.

Conclusion isn't easy but I'm clear,
What Homer wrote is very, very dear.

Horace

His childhood home Venusia he would leave
    When auctioneer father saw the chance;
Then lessons from Orbilius he'd receive,
And leaving Rome to Athens would advance.

He took to Brutus' cause at Philippi,
Though when things failed he dropped his shield and ran.
Once pardoned, back in town, he'd occupy
An office in accounts, a sorry man.

On meeting Virgil once, he was awestruck
By epic skill, the substance of his trade.
Maecenas saw his artistry – what luck!
Gave Sabine villa, just what he had prayed.

Augustus wanted him as secretary.
Our poet? Horace? No! That couldn't be.

Juvenal

An angry man? Well maybe so. He wrote
Of folly, faults and vice all swirling round.
But satire was a Roman thing, to quote,
And Juvenal took place in the foreground.

Domitian's mullet's slated in his verse
Along with swollen Tiber from the horde:
Indignant at the wealthy, he'd disperse
His savagery on them as kind reward.

Reality was his, no tales of gods:
His sixteen satires, lampoons and attacks.
Aristocratic folks and nobby bods
Clear in his sights, were ones would feel his axe.

But country ways and noble poverty,
Admired by him, kept free from mockery.

Livy

Augustus' chum was one-time Paduan chap,
Whose love for letters led him on to write
A hundred tomes or more. That's hardly scraps!
Cast doughty deeds of Rome in his limelight.

Emergent sources of this early state
Appealed to eager readers of his scrolls.
The first twin king and final Tarquin's fate,
The monarchy collapsed, replaced by polls.

Once Hannibalic elephantine Alps
Attracted Livy's interest and his pen:
Then Gaulish aims to take some Roman scalps,
As Archimedes' engines faced their men.

Didactic purpose always his, it seems.
Romantic stories showcased Livy's dreams.

Lucretius

*I*f Epicurus said you'd not come back,
    Then maybe you'd incline to hear his view.
The natural way to die and not backtrack,
Gives guilt-free clearance, anything you do.

Your soul will go when you do, said this chap,
And everything you do is just material.
Unpunished when you die, there is no trap
In which to fall, when you become ethereal.

We're made of atoms swarming round in space:
Though some collide, they're never really fixed.
Don't fear nor fret what comes. When once this race
Is done, it's done, and all offences nixed.

Free will is just your thing when atoms swerve:
Well, anyway, that's in Lucretius' oeuvre.

Martial

The Bilbilid was always poor. That's what
He said. Well, maybe so. I can't oppose
The Bilbilid and say it's really not
What he once said, or try to interpose.

He said he wasn't rich on his third floor:
He wrote for cash, though what I find quite funny,
His insults surely might have made him poor,
If all his insultees had sued for money.

Invented names were maybe his cop-out,
Concealing those whose meanness he'd attack.
But drunkards, gluttons, even thieves pop out
For payoffs after slanderous wisecracks.

He made us laugh. No, makes us laugh now still.
Whose epigrams, for some, a bitter pill.

Ovid

He wrote of heroes, monsters and of gods;
The changes of his tales would entertain.
Once Echo and Narcissus fell at odds,
And Icarus his dad did cause great pain.

Augustus sent him off to Black Sea coast:
A poem and a blunder's cause for that.
He hated Tomis exile, whipping-post
Became, self-pitying, sad, caveat.

Well what that blunder was is cause for doubt,
Though many take their chance to speculate.
(Imperial daughter's exile came about
Around the time of naughty poet's fate.)

He wrote of heroes, monsters and of gods,
Who died abroad and stayed, against the odds.

Pheidias

C hryselephantine statues flabbergast
   And when you have them made, you'll need a wad.
The gold and ivory mixture's unsurpassed,
And specially reserved for temple god.

When our man made his Zeus at sporting ground,
Perhaps he dreamt it, wonder of the world.
Which athletes, runners, jumpers might astound
And those who boxed and wrestled, discus hurled.

On Parthenon his frieze would win high praise:
Athena's statues tall and high would gleam.
At sculptor's skill the citizens would gaze,
Admiring man with Periclean dream.

A gold emblezzer, he? Not likely so.
Just used it all on statues, apropos.

Plato

It's Plato's theories dominate the scene,
    When philosophical debate comes round.
On education, art and things unseen,
His ideas, lofty, raise us from the ground.

Symposium? A party book to read:
Two halves of lovers split in endless quest.
Like crabs they scuttle, roused up in their need,
To find the parts once severed from the rest.

His Socrates was always on the ask,
With questions framed in clear opacity.
Distinguishing those dialogues, set task
For founder, Head of the Academy.

His theories top the board, but when it came
To bullseye Dionysius? Misaim.

Pliny

Not one but two will feature in this verse.

There's elder, uncle, natural history buff:

Volcano's observation was his curse;

Pompeian party, portly, out of puff.

His nephew was the younger, wrote the letters,

To all and sundry round the Roman world;

To writers, politicians and go-getters,

His views on life and all that stuff unfurled.

Book Ten perhaps his best, sent off to Trajan.

Who told him just exactly what to do,

When fighting fires or dealing with contagion,

Or working out a policy review.

This brace of Plinys left us loads of text,

Though which was which can sometimes leave us vexed.

Pythagoras

A squared plus B squared is C squared. So what?
Pythagoras is still the way to go.
In geometry his theorem's still hot;
Hypotenuses calculated so.

A polymath whose —ism seems quite strange,
His followers left Samos in his train.
His mystic meanings, numbers in a range,
Which universe disclosed, despite arcane.

His view on souls are rather less than sound:
On hearing beaten puppy howl in pain,
He said he recognised from puny hound,
His dead friend's voice, come back, restored again.

So is it fair to quote his golden thigh?
That kind of nonsense makes me want to sigh.

Seneca

*D*on't blame the teacher! Say that loud and clear!
  Your dodgy pupils don't get it from you!
If once they stray, it's not your fault, my dear,
And Nero was a bad one through and through.

Consoling Seneca might go like that,
Though frankly, stoic fortitude's his thing.
So maybe if you'd stopped to have a chat,
He might have said, his charge malfunctioning.

He tried so hard with Burrus to control
The young man's ways of thinking, morals too.
His letters and his precepts still cajole,
Encouraging a better me and you.

High morals, lofty ideals, dignified
With admiration, brave man's suicide.

Sophocles

When victory after Salamis was won,
A Chorus rose and sang the paean's strain.
Its leader, youthful lad, Athenian;
His future yet undreamt would swamp refrain.

He treated noble themes: the lives he wrote
Not as they were but as they ought to be.
Two dozen times his winning anecdotes
For Dionysian honour nominee.

Dramatic words translated yet resound:
Antigone and Ajax make us start;
Still Philoctetes' wounded foot astounds
His Oedipus remains his best-known part.

Both born and died in Athens, brought her fame:
A general twice, he served when crisis came.

Suetonius

He's just a gossip, Suetonius,

Who wrote the emperors' lives in Hadrian's pay;

Salacious, mendacious and erroneous,

Though frankly, very readable today.

His access to the records on the shelves

Was classified and cleared, so he could read

The letters and the notes they'd made themselves.

There's nothing that he hadn't got he'd need.

The problem with this author is, you see,

His master wanted others to seem worse

Than him: promoting eccentricity

His mission yardstick. Facts and truth diverse.

Sabina with her man to Britain came,

Whence writer was despatched in unknown shame.

Tacitus

Keep it short! Someone must have said to him,
Since brevity's a worthy thing to note.
Change things about a bit but always skim
Uncalled for flotsam from your anecdote.

Domitian's damned with varied eloquence,
Though politicians always hedge their bets.
Germanicus admired, his eminence
Brought low by Piso's poison, with regret.

Agricola, while heralded a hero,
His family connections cast a doubt.
But when it came to others such as Nero,
Cornelius showed contempt and scourged all-out.

To end this ode, a Tacitean thought:
Write anything you like: just keep it short!

Thucydides

In holding back the raids of Brasidas,
The general sent to Thrace would not prevail.
Amphipolis was lost in that impasse;
A new career was needed now he'd failed.

Thucydides decided he would pen
The story of the fighting he'd once tried.
With accurate accounts, he'd start again,
He'd analyse the strengths on either side.

His Great War stories often strike a chord,
Since he believed the past could teach us now.
Possession for all time he called his words;
Romantic stuff in stories too low-brow.

His tireless research means he's never vague.
Was so committed, even tested plague.

Virgil

He's surely golden boy of Roman verse,
Who gave us greatest epic of his time?
Adopted by Maecenas to disburse
Proud poems for Augustus, in his prime.

The Eclogues were the first of three great hits:
The Georgics came along as number two;
Aeneid was his greatest show of wits,
That number three, which no-one else could do.

His Trojan hero had to leave the blaze,
With shouldered father and his son in hand:
To Carthage, where the lovestruck queen's wild ways
Would send him, under curse, to Latin land.

His Naples tomb still stands and will abide,
A mark for Rome's top poet, Dante's guide.

Socrates

Stars

of

State &

Standing

Agrippina

It's not the best of starts in life maybe,

    To be the sister of Caligula.

Though none could quite predict or yet foresee

The depths to which she'd sink, this monstrous star.

If lecher brother's incest's not quite right,

Well how about an uncle ripe to pluck?

She lured old Claudius on in open sight,

His son Britannicus, right out of luck.

Then after mushrooms, hubby came to croak

And nasty Nero found top job reward.

Before so very long he did revoke

Opposing heads on coins he'd not afford.

Once mummy, groped, would board his special boat,

Her fate was sealed: she'd never stay afloat.

Alcibiades

The golden boy of Athens once did bite
    His eager foe while battling in the street.
The taunt rose, *Like a woman in the fight,*
Though he replied, *A lion.* (His conceit.)

His teams of horses won Olympic crowns:
Commander's victories thick and fast were took.
Though once the balls from herms got lopped, those frowns
Success Sicilian couldn't overlook.

Then changing sides, as Sparta's admiral,
He took the war out east and won more days.
Democracy dismantled, radical,
Returned to Athens, only just a phase.

Shot down by Persians, far off, overseas;
Unworthy end for Alcibiades.

Alexander

Wise Aristotle taught him to be great,
Which Alexander strove for all his life.
Olympias' example? Maybe hate
For father Philip's long, unwanted strife.

The Macedonian lines he'd led, he'd take
To Issus, mighty Persian king did rout.
And then took Tyre before oasis break
In Egypt, where great city up would sprout.

It seemed he had a go but not a stop,
When on and on he led his men to war.
But when his ox-head horse once finally flopped,
His own career was nearly out the door.

Fair Bactrian girl Roxanne could never bear
A child for him. He died. Despair. No heir.

Arminius

They call him Hermann, source of German pride,
Who crushed three legions once in forest deep,
Who conned the Romans he was on their side;
First worked for Varus, then made governor weep.

He'd served the foreign master, learned his ways,
Apprenticed in the armies he'd attack.
He'd gained their trust and joined the equites,
Though all the time was planning key kick-back.

Out came report of raving rebel rampage;
Though just a sham, unleashed the Roman hordes;
When East across the Rhine they met an outrage,
Met Chauci, Marsi, Bructeri warlords.

In Rome, his head on wall Augustus cracked,
Kept on demanding, *Varus, legions back!*

Augustus

Dictator's dead, his body barely burned.

Vain question was, *Would people's power return?*

Off, Antony! Great nephew based his claim

On something special: use of Caesar's name.

Shared out the Roman world post-Philippi,

Took West while Antony took East thereby.

Then Cleopatra's lover, once hard-pressed

At Actium, would fail Agrippa's test.

Maecenas, prime persuader, authors' mate,

Spin doctor pilot, taught to tolerate.

Succession was a struggle he'd not win,

His wife had toxic plans for her own kin.

Ate fatal figs he'd grown upon his tree,

Revered, reluctant, first of dynasty.

Boudicca

When old King Prasutagus was no more,
His wife thought she could simply go along
As client queen for Romans like before:
Iceni lady surely got it wrong.

Invaders flogged her, took her maiden daughters,
With governor away in Anglesey.
Her bloodlust broke, the catalyst of slaughters,
As Anglian queen rose up in mutiny.

She fell on Colchester, then London town,
And then St Albans too, to cap the rest.
Destructive trail, she took the Romans down,
Until Paulinus came to check her quest.

Our Boudicca no Roman nonsense took:
The British girl they hoped to overlook.

Caligula

When little Gaius wore those little boots,
 Then little thought the Roman legionaries,
Germanicus's son, from Claudian roots,
Would drag degraded empire into sleaze.

Though hairy all around, he's bald on top,
Embarrassed by his scanty caprid coat.
A crime made capital, if one might pop
Above to stare or even mention goats.

Insane, or epileptic? Can't be proven:
His madness uncontrolled is definite.
Praetorians decided, would be prudent
To end his reign, would be no deficit.

He made his horse a senator, they say.
Though when he wanted motion, horse said *Neigh*.

Cincinnatus

Once, Lucius Quinctius, patriot, rescued Rome.
The Aequi tribesmen's threats had terrified
The citizens and senators; pressed home
That none but selfless yeoman unified.

He'd been their consul once before and served,
But once his office ended, went to plough
His fields and tend his crops: retired, unheard,
To work his farm as long as life allowed.

Though when they asked his help, his ploughshare struck
In earth, gave way, reluctantly conceded.
He picked up reins of power, still caked in muck,
To save the day in Algidus proceeded.

Once Lucius Quinctius, patriot, rescued Rome,
Gave up dictator's trappings, went back home.

Claudius

Caligula was dead and no one knew
If emperors had really had their day.
But when praetorian soldiers went into
The halls, protruding toes gave him away.

They needed a new figurehead, they vowed,
And corpse's uncle seemed to tick the box.
Not me, old Claudius objected loud,
But no one heard commanding paradox.

He stammered and he slobbered, had a tic;
He limped and lisped and people thought him dim.
Caught on, invaded Britain pretty quick,
And soon they saw a different kind of him.

The poor sap married monstrous Messallina,
But worse than her, assassin Agrippina.

Cleisthenes

A tyrant's grandson and aristocrat,
  Our Cleisthenes had doubts about his roots.
He rose to archon under Hippias,
But oligarchs, for him, lacked substitutes.

He cut his chart of Attica in three:
The coast, the city and the inland bits.
His so-called trittys took from them was key:
Three demes for each; all equal, as befits.

And then he added ten tribes to the mix:
Topography dictated all he'd brought.
So none could cheat the system, none could fix,
Assembly made the choices as it ought.

Democracy's inventor didn't spare:
Made people's power Athenian affair.

Cleopatra

Horatian fatal monster's comely charms
  Affected history more than some had thought.
First Caesar and then Antony disarmed,
As Egypt's queen her bold seductions wrought.

Though, to be fair, it can't have been much fun
To share her rule and marry little bro.
Not once but twice, you know, she'd had it done:
No wonder that she chose to overthrow.

Her golden goddess statue gave offence
In Rome's great temple by the Capitol.
Though worse by far the Actium suspense,
Her run for home with name now vitriol.

Octavian, when he was introduced,
Just gazed on her. Well, he'd not be seduced.

Constantine

Proclaimed *Augustus* by his troops in York,
He'd see his royal rank receive downgrade:
Galerius – Augustus true – would baulk:
He chose to call him *Caesar*, in a trade.

Then power-hungry Constantine fought long
And hard to win back his first epithet.
To Rome, where Milvian Bridge would see his throng
Aroused by Christian symbol: armies met.

He chose the ancient Nike as his emblem;
Pure messenger from God brought victory.
He moved the centre stage: Byzantium,
Where lasting end to infights he would see.

Right at the end, when feeling breath subside,
No time for sin, baptised before he died.

Hadrian

When Trajan's cousin coughed, he undertook
Protection of Paulina and her bro.
The Spanish boy on all things Greek got hooked
A love our *Graeculus* would not outgrow.

Promoted by Plotina, welcomed wife
Sabina seemed to suit as his new spouse;
Though years of disaffected married life
Would give apparent endless cause to grouse.

When Trajan died and power came to him,
There's plenty thought a dodgy deed was done.
But journeys round the empire doubts bedimmed:
With frontiers and a wall, his name was won.

Now Hadrian, though flawed, had great designs,
The architect who drafted Pantheon's lines.

Hadrian

Hannibal

*E*ternal hatred for that tribe you'll nurse!
    Now swear for me! The King of Carthage high
Made little Hannibal swear bitter curse
On Roman race, whose seed made Dido die.

From Spain he took his armies right up North;
His elephants through alpine passes drove.
Where Romans never thought that they'd break forth,
Right into sight at Trebia they hove.

Right up to Rome's great gates he forced his way,
Though never quite delivered mortal blow.
To Capua diverted; went astray,
Til Zama saw him meet a better foe.

Watch out! He'll have you! Stop! He's at the gates!
A bogeyman became, for reprobates.

Julia

*I*mperial daughters didn't have much fun,
If Julia's story shows how things were done...

Her mum Scribonia got divorced from dad,
When Livia's wiles took over lusty lad.

Marcellus was first husband: when he died,
Augustus put her on Agrippa's side.

Five children later, Actium's admiral
Conked out; saw her again, collateral.

Tiberius next her husband was to be,
Cementing dad and stepmum's families.

It's all too much to force a girl like this.
Must wed, must bed again? It's hardly bliss!

They banished her at last for being torrid;
Affair with poet Ovid thought too horrid.

Julius Caesar

Most famous of the Romans? Probably.
But call him emperor? I'd disagree.

When captured by the pirates, brought out boast:
He'd crucify the lot and make them toast.

Then triumvir and consul, off to Gaul.
Alesian attack? He built a second wall.

Brought troops to Britain twice, each time to leave;
Full occupation there he'd not achieve.

When Egypt's golden Venus woke desire,
Too much for Roman people, woke their ire.

Dictator for forever; that's the claim,
Which brought a final end to Caesar's game.

When daggers twenty three his flesh would prick,
Dictator fell. No more forever shtick.

Leonidas

Three hundred Spartans combed their hair that day,
    Outfaced by Xerxes near the heated gates.
When Persians asked them why, or so they say,
They claimed that death's not great with matted pates.

They knew they'd die but fought to buy Greece time,
So others could regroup to stop advance.
Two days they blocked the pass, til traitor's climb
Revealed a way for foes to take their chance.

A great black statue standing by the road
Reminds us still where fearless heroes stayed:
Those hot gates where Leonidas once strode,
High-helmeted and spear-up, unafraid.

That Spartan king died here, Thermopylae:
In shadow of those arrows in the sky.

Livia

At a party once, they say, off she fled
With young Octavian. Ears red, came back,
Dishevelled, damp, she smelt of sex and bed.
Which made the gossips round the table clack.

And even worse than that, perhaps, protruding
Bump a sign of other man. Her husband
Tiberius Claudius Nero, concluding
She'd dump, exchange the old for new, unmanned.

Augustus' wife, though childless from her catch,
Strove tireless to secure his future line.
Tiberius her son seemed her best match
To keep the Claudians out of a decline.

Marcellus, Gaius, Lucius? May have slain.
Germanicus, Agrippa? You explain!

Nero

Britannicus was easy prey for mum
To knock off perch and open up the way.
A dainty dish of mushrooms, daddy's done
And sonny-boy new emperor - her way.

He loved performing, dancing, singing, plays.
He'd make the senate take part in them too.
Though some would hate to watch and find mad ways
To make an exit, feign confinement new.

He built a house in gold, on stolen land
They said, the ashes of the fire still warm.
The punishment of Christians he'd demand,
Though many thought the blaze just him on form.

And when they warned him, *Rebels on the way,*
Not now, he said, *it's water organ day.*

Nero

Nicias

With wealth from silver's seam, quite upper class,
Came cautious, upright general Nicias.

Once Pericles' regime was done, expired,
Opposing warlike Cleon got him fired.

Amphipolis, a chance to set things straight:
An end to fighting then did legislate.

When Sicily called out, was unimpressed
With Alcibiades, on risky quest.

Yet one of three, was chosen, led the fleet
To Syracuse, where tried to stay discreet.

The Spartans came, then walls and cross-walls too:
Through all of it, he did what he must do.

Met cruel end, by Asinarus, hewn.
He could have run but feared the shaded moon.

Pericles

O nce prosecuted Cimon: ostracized;
　　　Reduced the power of Ares on his hill.
The leading democrat, in his disguise,
Ruled Athens and with greatness did instil.

The temples on the high top raise his name
On lips around the world, that's Pericles.
The Parthenon, majestic, still stakes claim
For finest architecture, if you please.

When plague-struck city felt the curse of war,
It turned against him, blamed him for the pest.
It stripped him of his rank in great uproar,
But reinstated later: *for the best.*

Came back, took charge, he spoke at the event:
Historic words, great city represent.

Pompey

When Sulla called and Pompey joined his trysts,
He stood against old Marius in the wars.
The triumph then was just his first on lists:
They called him *Great*, apparently with cause.

In Spain he held the day when rebel struck,
Returning second triumph back at home.
From Spartacus' revolt the glory plucked,
Left Crassus fuming all the way to Rome.

Expelled the pirates, took the Pontus prize,
His settlement would truly fix the East.
Third triumph now, his star up high in skies,
Though Senate's blessing failed him in the feast.

As one of three, he joined in Caesar's club.
He lost his head in Egypt; quite a snub.

Sabina

Her braided hair, her elegance, exudes
From statues in museums round the globe.
With beauty and quiet calm, it all alludes
To perfect empress, perfect in her robe.

Sophisticated charm, all very well:
Sabina wouldn't really be like this.
Know Hadrian's her husband. Once the swell
Of first love burst, she didn't feel much bliss.

Her rival's young, her rival's just a boy,
A Turkish lad, though handsome right enough.
It's Antinous the lad, the rival joy,
Who made her life at home so very tough.

Affair in Britain? Should have stayed in Rome.
Her husband's spies were bribable back home.

Sabina

Sejanus

When number one's away, it's time to play
For number two, or that's the story here.
If old Tiberius wasn't émigré
In Capri, he'd have never ruled with fear.

Sejanus was the perfect prefect til
He thought of sending Drusus down below:
With poison, seemingly, he went for kill,
And wife Livilla tempted for trousseau.

Tiberius was old and foolish: yet
Once trusted chum, now known, he planned to snare:
The old lieutenant captured in his net,
Would pay for crimes he never should have dared.

His letter, read in Senate, got their vote.
Sejanus, torn apart, was left to float.

Socrates

His ugly face was known in every street,
    The man who stopped to ask the time of day,
Then asked more things, while folk stood shuffling feet,
Just wondering when he would go away.

Can good be learned? Is Justice real? What's death?
His questions barely stopped. But that's the knack!
The answers made life living, gave it breath,
But like the gadfly, some would want to whack.

When Delphic riddle answered wisest quest,
He said he lacked the knowledge it would prove.
I know I only don't know was his jest:
If played for laughs, it didn't really move.

They charged him at the end, *corrupted youth;*
Who took the hemlock, only sought the truth.

Solon

The poor grew poorer, yet the rich stayed rich:
Draconian laws Athenians distressed;
From debts excessive, self and freedom switched;
The citizens, by slavery repressed.

He cancelled all collateral of self,
Abolished debt's dependent liberty.
The burdens of the poor now on the shelf,
The rich must find a new security.

Those immigrants would thank him for his fights,
Whose craftsmanship would help economy.
New citizens took heart from their new rights:
His greatest gift to those folks, they'd stay free.

The great reformer spoke to my concern:
Yet you grow old, you still can always learn.

Sulla

Though Marius taught him craft, it's not the same
For people's party and the Optimates.
They drift apart then come to war – for shame!
Well, Mithridates sealed the fighters' fates.

The consul marched on Rome to sort things out,
Which none had done before, nor ever should.
Proscribed the ones opposed in his stakeout;
Retired from public life, was gone for good.

Dictators pass and sometimes it's not nice
To write about their dreadful dying days.
But Sulla's case is different, my advice,
'Cos *Lucky* really went out in a blaze.

His gory end? He got his just returns:
His meat and muscle munched up by the worms.

Tiberius

Augustus chose his heirs but none survived:
It's hard to think old Livia wasn't prone
To poison. When old man died, she'd contrived
Her son's advancement to his stepdad's throne.

He'd never really wanted much at all,
Save left alone to love Vipsania.
Was forced to dump her, ran to Rhodes, recalled,
Escaped his unsought spouse, spoiled Julia.

The vile old goat left town, Capri now home.
A cruel, perverted life that he would lead.
Sejanus power abused, offended Rome,
Until, exposed and bloody, he'd concede.

Who never saw himself as emperor,
Got smothered at the end: Caligula.

Trajan

The next time that I visit Rome, I will!
I'll stand and gaze, in awe. (I always do.)
Those carvings on the column rise uphill
And Trajan's great adventures play right through.

Decebalus is there with curving blade,
About to slit his throat in his defeat.
While on the platform, emperor with aides
Dispatches troops to battle, the elite.

The ships that cross the Danube line up there,
As Neptune gazes on in kindly mood.
The towers guard the transports and declare
To enemies that Romans have them screwed.

And still the Dacian foe are trampled down:
Still serried ranks of Romans gain renown.

Vespasian

This Flavian first was humble from the off:
A blunt and ugly sort of chap, it's true.
Unlike the other emperors, he's no toff,
But struggled hard and earned his great breakthrough.

When Claudius came to Britain, kept in line
With other soldiers making new frontiers.
Judea's desert troops he'd reassign
Before the revolution's new ideas.

Once boss in Rome, this gruff but cheerful cove
Would start to plan the stadium of his dreams.
With Colosseum's architecture, strove
To publicise his Flavian regime.

That smelly urine joke was quite a line:
While last breath dwindled, thought himself divine.

INDEX OF STARS

ALSO AVAILABLE

SONNETS FOR YORKSHIRE STARS

The poems in this collection have been written to celebrate 100 of the county's outstanding achievers. The list of their names was compiled carefully to reflect all aspects of life, so you'll find artists, musicians, politicians, sporting personalities and writers here: Yorkshire's finest, all celebrated in fourteen-line verse.

"So honoured that you chose to write of me and am delighted it was in the form of a poem and not a puzzle! Warmest good wishes."
Baroness Betty Boothroyd

"reet grand"
Alastair Campbell

"I feel flattered to be portrayed in verse."
Peter Wright, The Yorkshire Vet

"Many thanks. Very interesting to read about my fellow Yorkshire folk."
Dickie Bird

"The sonnet is a hard form to pull off and to pull off well. Sometimes the form overwhelms the content and sometimes the content struggles to do justice to the form but these sonnets hit the nail on the head, telling perfectly crafted stories that brim with rhythm and dance with rhyme."
Ian McMillan

"A genuinely surprising and novel idea. Julian has succeeded in encapsulating the lives and achievements of dozens of Yorkshire greats, creating bite-sized biographies in the style of a Shakespearean sonnet."
Adrian Braddy, Editor, Dalesman

For further details, see www.yorkshireauthor.com

LATIN AND GREEK PUZZLE BOOKS

These collections are aimed at those who want to have some fun with the Latin and Greek languages they know and love. All of these books feature solutions at the back, for those who get stuck.

Easy Latin Puzzles was written after compiling three lists of words commonly used in a variety of Latin courses. It makes very limited use of word endings and includes a variety of challenges, including sudokus, word searches, Latin to English crosswords and English to Latin ones. The book features the full word lists at the back.

Tricky Latin Puzzles was written for students learning Latin today or for those to whom the good old days beckon. These 50 crossword puzzles, sudokus, wordsearches and other brainteasers should bring plenty of fun. It is aimed at those who have studied the language for two or three years at least.

Easy Greek Puzzles is a collection of 50 brainteasers, assembled from two short lists of words commonly used in a variety of courses. It uses all five cases of noun, adjective and pronoun systems and active indicative verb endings from the present, imperfect, aorist and future tenses. As such, it is appropriate for use by those who have studied the language for around one year or longer. It features sudokus, word searches, Greek to English crosswords and English to Greek ones.

Tricky Greek Puzzles was written for those whose command of ancient Greek may allow them to enjoy its challenges - not for the faint-hearted. It includes 50 crosswords, sudokus, wordsearches and other brainteasers and is aimed at those who have studied the language for two or three years at least.

For further details, see www.j-progs.com

120

CLASSICAL PUZZLES

Classical Puzzles is a collection of brainteasers which focuses on the literature, culture and history of the ancient world rather than its languages. There are many people fascinated by classical civilisation who have not studied Latin and Greek and up until now, they may have been denied some fun: this book is an attempt to put that right and to complement my existing range of Latin and Greek puzzle books, not to mention the Yorkshire ones.

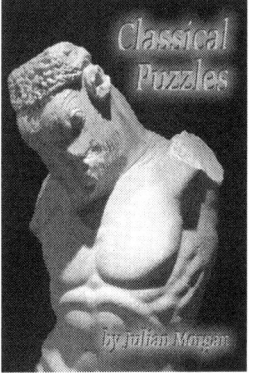

This collection will test your knowledge of the Greeks and Romans to the max, with crosswords, sudokus and all kinds of wordgames to challenge you. Go on, test yourself out.

Can you separate your Caesars from your Ciceros? Your Spartans from your Athenians? It's all here: from art and architecture to geography, from politics to literature, from history to myths; a cornucopia of classical civilisation!

WORLD OF JAMES HERRIOT PUZZLES

World of James Herriot Puzzles features 50 puzzles, aligned closely to the original eight books of memoirs by the world's most famous vet. The book should put even the most ardent Herriot fans to the test: animals and ailments, colleagues and customers, potions and powders of the original eight books of memoirs are all here, as well as on-screen portrayals of vets and locations, both real and fictional. But don't worry: if it all gets too much, the solutions are in the back.

"Julian's puzzles are respectful in adhering to the original stories and will bring new ways for readers to connect again with the stories they love."

Ian Ashton, Managing Director, World of James Herriot

For further details, see www.yorkshireauthor.com

IMPERIUM LATIN COURSE

The Imperium Latin course was written for the twenty-first century; unique, highly resourced and written to make fullest use of modern technology. Its texts follow the life of the Emperor Hadrian from his early childhood to his later years, as he became the most powerful man in the Roman world.

Imperium was released for general use in 2013, after a trialling period of six years. It consists of three course books, a Grammar and Syntax book, a puzzle book and the Imperium Latin Unseens collection for advanced users. All of these texts can be ordered through Amazon but are also available as pdf files in our Site Support Packs, which can be bought by schools. The three course books are also available as free of charge downloadable pdf files, from the TES Resources website.

For further details, see www.imperiumlatin.com

ABOUT THE AUTHOR

Julian Morgan was born in the West Riding, brought up in the East Riding, and currently lives in North Yorkshire. He served as a teacher and a Head of Classics for many years in the UK, before taking up a post in 2007 at the European School of Karlsruhe in Germany. Julian recently stepped down from classroom teaching and is beginning to rediscover his great love of his native Yorkshire.

Julian has written many educational software titles and books in the last 25 years, publishing most of them under the banner of **J-PROGS**. His Imperium Latin course is used in a good number of schools and can be downloaded free of charge from www.imperiumlatin.com. Julian has spent much of his recent time developing books of puzzles and sonnets on both Yorkshire and classical themes.

He can often be found walking his dog in the Great Wold Valley of North Yorkshire, where he lives.

Please visit these links to find out more:

www.yorkshireauthor.com

Twitter feed: @yorkshireauthor

31861599R00076

Printed in Poland
by Amazon Fulfillment
Poland Sp. z o.o., Wrocław